Chicken Soup
for the Soul

Giving
Thanks

Amy Newmark

CSS

Chicken Soup for the Soul, LLC
Cos Cob, CT

Chicken Soup for the Soul: Giving Thanks
Amy Newmark

Published by Chicken Soup for the Soul, LLC www.chickensoup.com

The publisher gratefully acknowledges the many publishers and individuals who granted Chicken Soup for the Soul permission to reprint the cited material.

Front cover and interior photo courtesy of iStockPhoto.com/TimeFoto (© TimeFoto).

Interior photo of Amy Newmark courtesy of Susan Morrow at SwickPix

Cover and Interior by Daniel Zaccari

ISBN: 978-1-61159-062-3

Table of Contents

My Epiphany

With the past, I have nothing to do; nor
with the future. I live now.
~Ralph Waldo Emerson

t seems that when something awful happens to me, my mind just shuts down. These things change the way I think for a period of time after they happen. Somehow, I find a way to keep it all together by reverting to my "one day at a time" motto, but really, inside, I'm freaking out. Sometimes I'm freaking out and I don't even realize it yet. I've discovered lately that moving on from those difficult times really is a process.

These days, I am in the final stages of my long battle with osteosarcoma, a bone cancer, which made its appearance when I was fourteen years old, claimed one of my lower legs and a lung along the way, and recently spread to my brain. The doctors found three or four new tumors in my brain. This news was a terrible blow since it meant two huge things. It meant that one, along with the nodules that I already had in my single lung, the Thalidomide I have been trying isn't doing a single thing for me. And secondly it officially marked me as terminal. The doctors told us that they thought I probably had less than a month to live.

It has now been longer than a month, and I am still here and still feeling well. Nothing has truly changed about my situation. I am still taking medication for the headaches, and sometimes my breathing is a lot more strained than it used to be. Although I do have a cold, which could be part of it, it's most likely that the cancer *is* progressing. There is nothing in my situation that has changed. I know that I probably won't make it, still. But there is something different now about the way I look at things. I *feel* different. I feel inspired! I feel invigorated! I don't feel like I'm just sitting around waiting to die anymore. I feel infused with life. There's a reason I have already beaten the odds. There's a reason it's not time yet.

I don't know what came first—the changes to my daily routine, or the changes to my perspective. But somehow they're working together to be just what I needed. During the past week or so we've been making small changes to my medications since I've been doing so well. The first thing we did was drop the nausea medicine I'd been taking on a schedule with the pain medication. It turns out that I don't really need it at all, since I haven't had any nausea since. We also started weaning me off the steroid I'd been taking to control swelling, which makes me eat everything in sight and makes me swell up like a balloon. Somehow, and the only thing I can think to attribute it to, is that by getting rid of those two medications, I am feeling a little more like myself. I haven't had to take a nap in ages! My eyes, which had been blurry and unfocused, are doing so well that I finished a book that I was reading... on my Kindle! My computer screen no longer tries to flip letters around. But that's not all—a few days ago Mom convinced me to put my prosthetic leg on for a while. It didn't take too much cajoling, since it was something I'd been meaning to try since I have been feeling better. It doesn't quite fit right because I haven't worn it in a month. Right now because I haven't been wearing it, I have no leg muscle to even hardly hold it up. But I can kind of walk on it, with my crutches, and I have hope and faith that before long I'll be able to use it again for a short time. :)

I'm not sure where it came from, this sudden epiphany I've had. But something inside me has clicked. It reminds me of a story my pastor told me when he came by for a visit, about a man who was pronounced terminal. Another person asked him, "What are you doing right now?" And the man who was dying answered, "Well I'm terminal, I'm dying." The first man either asked him again what he was doing right now or informed him somehow that he was wrong. The man who was terminal wasn't dying just then, just at that moment he was living. And as long as he was breathing he would be living. That's the epiphany I've had. Right now, regardless of the things to come, I'm living! I'm not sitting around waiting to die. My entire perspective has changed. I'm alive right now. I'm living.

So, today I leave you with this message, one that I can hardly believe that I went this far without. Cherish every single day. It is one of those things that is easier said than done. The way that something feels is all about perspective. Sometimes our hearts don't need a miracle. Sometimes there just aren't any miracles and the world around us feels like there can never be any happiness in it again. I know how that feels. I have had some dark days these last few months. I won't lie. It's difficult to know that eventually I won't feel good. It's hard to know that essentially I'm just sitting around waiting for the cancer to progress.

I can't think like that anymore. I have to think about the things that I can do. The life that I can live. I may not be able to go on the ski trip this month, but I'm still doing better than expected. I'm still here. I'm still living. Life is precious, whether you have a straight road stretched before you as far as the eye can see, or whether, like most people, your road turns and bends into the undergrowth and you have no idea where it leads. Follow that bend, and your heart, no matter where it goes. Mine may go on, to places unmentionable, but everyone's does, eventually. All roads lead to the same bend, and although we can't see around the corner, I know there are people who have gone before me that will help me when I get there. But for now, I'm not there yet. Today I'm living, and my heart sings with joy for the days that follow.

For anyone going through a difficult time, I want to pass on the list of ten steps that I composed. These steps have helped me move forward in the past. I'm not a professional and I have no claim to fame, but these steps have helped me and I want to share them with other people. Here are my Ten Steps to Moving Forward:

1. Cry, Yell, and Grieve: The first step can make you feel like you are taking a few steps back, but it is necessary. I think when something happens that reroutes your entire life and the direction you were going previously, it is normal to grieve and be sad. Because I believe that whenever you go through a difficult time, it changes you. It changes the way you think and perceive things, and the first step to acceptance of the new reality, whatever it is, is to mourn the past and the person you used to be. So, let yourself grieve for as long as you need to, and when you're able, you'll find the next step.

2. Talk When You're Ready: Sometimes you feel like talking things through and sometimes you don't. When you're ready to talk, find someone who you can talk to as an equal and whose opinion you value, and pour your heart out. Sometimes, just having someone who cares and who is there for you, no matter what, gives you the boost you need, to move on from the first step (even though you may feel still the need to grieve from time to time).

3. Escape When You Need To: but not too often. Sometimes life just takes a dump on you, and your heart and mind are too full to process things in a healthy way. In these moments, escape is essential; watch a TV show or movie, read a book, or veg out on the Internet. Take a break from the things that are weighing you down, and come back to them later with a fresh outlook. But I caution you on escaping too often, because escaping never makes your problems go away, and you always have to deal with them eventually.

4. Start Small: If the big things are too overwhelming at any given moment, start small. Instead of worrying about a huge appointment next week that you're afraid might hold bad news (perhaps similar to where you just were) try to focus on smaller more attainable goals. Rather than brooding about the appointment, focus on your exercises, your chores, or even your homework assignments. You'll get there in the same amount of time, whether or not you worry about it.

5. Find Your Muse: Your muse is the source of your inspiration. Find the thing, or things, that inspire you the most, and absorb them into your world. These could be anything. For some, it could be their children, others music or nature, and for people like me, poetry or literature.

6. Reach Out: Interaction is an important thing in any person's life. Reaching out doesn't necessarily mean telling everyone about your struggles, rather it means finding people you enjoy, and spending time with them. It can mean laughing and teasing each other, but it also means support. Maybe not support like that of step two, but support that lets you know that they care and that they're thinking of you. This kind of support is a bulwark that can bolster you through any storm. These are the people who know how to cheer you on, when you're going through a hard time.

7. Channel Your Nervous Energy: Often you may find yourself stressing out and worrying. The best way to prevent this is to throw yourself headlong into another project, albeit a more relaxing one. For me, this usually means writing, scrapbooking, or artwork of some kind. I actually find that some of my best poetry is written when I'm trying not to freak out.

8. Help Someone Else: Helping someone else is actually a great way to help you deal with tough things that are going on your own life. It may sound selfish, in an ironic way. But not only does helping someone through their problems distract you, it also fills you with a pleasant satisfaction. Plain and simple; it feels good to help someone else out.

9. Focus on the Good Things: If you go through life with a "woe is me" attitude, things can seem harder than they really are. Granted, I'm finding that optimism comes more easily to me than most, but I cannot help but feel that some optimism is imperative to dealing with any situation. By focusing on the good things in your life, you can muster up enough strength to hope. And I believe that hope is ultimately what allows you to move on.

10. Take One Day At a Time: We spend so much time worrying about things that are far in the future, that we miss the things that are happening in the moment. Even if the moment you are in seems difficult, and there are things on the horizon that seem even more difficult, it is important to focus on the moment you are in. We can't worry about things that haven't happened yet, or that may or may not happen. If you must worry, worry about the day you are in, and worry about tomorrow, well, tomorrow. But remember also, no matter what you're going through, that you will get through. No matter how hard it seems in that moment, or how bleak the future looks, time will move you forward against your will. Eventually you'll find that things don't seem as hard, or hurt as bad, and life will take on a new routine. And you'll be okay. Or... at least that's the way it's been for me.

~Angela Sayers

The Great Thanksgiving Challenge

I can no other answer make,
but, thanks, and thanks.
~William Shakespeare

My friend Marilyn and I had just settled into a booth at our favorite coffee shop. "BookTalk is at my house next month," I said. "I hate getting ready for it."

"I know what you mean," Marilyn answered. "I spent a week cleaning when it was my turn in

February, not to mention baking two cakes."

"Not to mention that it's all over in a couple of hours. All that work for two hours!"

Marilyn nodded as we sipped from steaming cups of latte.

"And if that's not bad enough," I said, wiping foam from my upper lip, "my entire family is coming for Thanksgiving this year. I love them dearly, but you know what that means?"

"Yep. Cooking and cleaning, changing sheets, wondering what to feed everybody for breakfast. I go through the same thing every year."

The chimes on the coffee shop door jingled and a bedraggled woman entered, carrying two super-sized shopping bags stuffed with odds and ends. Twists of gray hair escaped from the ratty scarf covering her head. Nothing she wore matched, and one black canvas high top had a hole at the big toe. As she passed us, it was evident she hadn't bathed in days.

"Would you listen to us?" I whispered, feeling ashamed of myself. "We sound like two ungrateful curmudgeons."

"That poor woman probably can't pay for a cup of coffee."

"Do you think she's homeless?" I asked.

Marilyn shrugged her shoulders. Then she grabbed her wallet, and headed for the counter where she paid for the woman's coffee and an apple fritter. The woman smiled, showing bad teeth. I heard Marilyn invite her to join us, but the woman shook her head and settled into a soft chair in a sunlit corner of the shop.

"That was nice," I said when Marilyn slid back into the booth.

She rolled her eyes. "That was guilt."

I nibbled a piece of chocolate biscotti. "You know something? Some days, all I do is complain."

"Me, too."

"Take BookTalk for instance. Those women are smart and funny. I'm honored they asked me to join the club. The last thing I should do is complain about having them come to my house for a few hours."

Marilyn glanced at the woman thumbing through a tattered *People* magazine. "I don't know why I always see the glass half empty when it's more than half full," she said.

"We should stop complaining—it's a bad habit." I said this with more conviction than I felt.

Marilyn set her cup down just as a megawatt smile broke over her face.

"What?" I asked.

When Marilyn gets that look, it always means some bold plan has taken hold of her brain—usually one that includes me.

"We'll give it up. Complaining. We'll give it up for Thanksgiving."

"You mean Lent. That's months away."

"No—I mean we'll stop complaining and start being thankful. Just in time for Thanksgiving. It takes thirty days to drop a habit and thirty days to start a new one."

"So what's your plan?"

Marilyn leaned back and crossed her arms. "A

challenge. We'll keep a diary. Write down every complaint. Then think of something to be thankful for, and write that down too."

"What if we can't think of something to be thankful for?"

Marilyn pointed to the old woman who had fallen asleep in her chair. "You can think of something."

"Then how will we know we're really keeping track? It would be easy to cheat."

Marilyn stuck out her little finger. Now it was my turn to roll my eyes. Pinky swear. We'd been doing it since junior high.

"Challenge accepted," I said.

Thanksgiving Day was a month and a half away. Could we really drop a bad habit by then? And replace it with a new one?

The next morning I poured my cereal and picked up the milk carton only to discover it was empty.

"I can't eat cereal without milk," I muttered. Then I caught myself, not believing the first words out of my mouth that day took the form of a complaint.

"Great," I said, talking to the cat. "Can't even start the day right."

And there it was: complaint number two.

"This is going to be harder than I thought," I said, searching the desk shelves for a notebook. "Why can't I ever find what I need when I need it?"

Welcome to my world, complaints three and four.

I grabbed the phone and dialed Marilyn's number.

"What's up?" she asked, way too perky for early morning.

"I've been awake fifteen minutes and all I've done is complain," I complained. "This is hard!"

"No kidding. Jim forgot to make the coffee last night—his job—and I had to wait ten minutes for the pot to brew."

"Did you write that down?"

Marilyn laughed. "Can't find a notebook."

"Neither can I!"

"Okay—quick—what are you thankful for?" she asked.

"I'm talking on the phone with my best friend and the cat is purring in my lap. What about you?"

"I'm drinking coffee in a warm kitchen and about to go work out," Marilyn answered. "See? This won't be so hard after all."

But it was hard. Hard to believe I complained so much about trivial things. Hard to believe I wasn't more thankful for my family, my friends, and my health. My mind kept wandering back to the homeless woman, and I caught myself saying little prayers for her.

BookTalk met at my house the first week of November. In preparation, I cleaned and cooked and complained. But I recorded the blessings, too: my husband cheerfully moved furniture to accommodate thirty women; the cheesecakes I baked were perfect; my friends in the book club complimented my beautiful home—and I realized they were right.

As weeks passed, I noticed my notebook recorded more blessings than complaints. Marilyn reported the same phenomenon. That's not to say we didn't complain—we did. Just not as much. Maybe the complaints dwindled because we realized we had so much to be thankful for.

The Monday after Thanksgiving, Marilyn and I met for coffee again, comparing stories of the holiday weekend and sharing what we'd written in the pages of our notebooks.

"It's interesting," Marilyn said. "I don't complain as much now. And when I do, the complaints sound more like problem statements than whining."

"I feel better about myself, too. And about life in general." I took a sip of creamy latte. "I guess we owe that homeless woman a bushel of gratitude, don't we?"

"Yeah," Marilyn said. "We sure do."

~Ruth Jones

Finding My Joy

Joy is a flower that blooms when you do.
~Author Unknown

I have a confession to make. I lose things all the time. You know my type. I'm the lady who drives out of the restaurant parking lot with her take-out on the roof of the car. The one who leaves the windows open during thunderstorms. The one who needs three duplicate sets of keys hidden in rocks and crevices all over her property.

By now I've even lost track of how many things I've lost.

I'd like to blame it on the fact that I'm a mom to six children. Or to pretend it's the stress of home-schooling that causes my forgetfulness. Plus, I've got the added responsibilities that come with being a pastor's wife. All good reasons, don't you think? But the truth is, I was this way long before we married, started a family, entered the ministry or taught the first home-school lesson.

If you ran into me on the street, you'd never guess I'm so scatterbrained. I can do a pretty good imitation of competence. But chances are I'm probably standing there doing a figurative head scratch while I ask myself the question: What was I doing again?

See what I mean? Even my train of thought gets lost.

People like me need a strategy for coping with such forgetfulness, and I've developed an excellent one, if I do say so myself. It's very simple. I never panic when something goes missing and I never look for it. My theory, however unscientific, is that it will turn up the minute I stop searching for it.

Library books, driver's license, car keys, cell phone, birth certificate, wallet, plane tickets—you name it, I've lost it. I've also found every single item, because eventually this stuff resurfaced. Granted, sometimes it took as long as three years, but still. I found the things I lost. Every time. Without fail.

My theory worked like a charm.

Until the day it didn't. That was the day I lost something and couldn't find it again.

I lost my joy.

As usual, I waited a while for it to return. But as the weeks passed, I began to panic. I wondered how long it would be before I felt happy again. In place of light, there was darkness. Anxiety rooted in my heart where contentment used to live.

As the weeks turned into long months, I struggled to ignore the depression that was bearing down and smothering me. I knew it was one of those things women may experience after childbirth, but my baby was six months old. Exercise, sunshine, even a trip to my doctor wasn't helping my heavy heart. Given that I used to look forward to each new day, this change was a hard pill to swallow.

I tried to grit my teeth and power through until the fog lifted and the burden eased. After all, everyone has bad days now and then, right? In the meantime, I spent a lot of time sitting on the bathroom floor, leaning against the tub and crying while the bath water ran.

I had to do something.

So I did the one thing I'd never done before, and went out in search of what I'd lost.

I started by closing my eyes and praying for joy. Only then did I begin to see where it had been hiding. It was first spotted in the pages of my Bible. Then later, I found it in the rocking chair with my baby in my lap, and even more when I felt my toddler's arms around my neck.

The fog began to lift. After that, when I learned how to say no, the clouds cleared and the sun came out. I realized my older children didn't have to be in organized sports if it meant extra stress. My seven-year-old could learn Spanish in high school as opposed to the first grade. The house didn't have to be perfectly clean. I could let go of the smaller things to gain much greater things.

Little by little, it came back.

Joy.

Contentment.

Peace.

And a truly grateful heart.

Of course, I still lose things all the time. Just the other day I lost a prescription on the way to get it filled, the dog's medication, and the check register.

I still use my old theory and say with a shrug, "Eh. It'll resurface eventually."

But I use my new theory, too. I search with eyes shut and hands folded in prayer.

Because if it's really something I need, I know God will bring it back to me.

~Debra Mayhew

My Own
Happiness Project

*Happiness is an attitude. We either make
ourselves miserable, or happy and strong.
The amount of work is the same.*
~Francesca Reigler

When you find yourself sobbing unexpectedly in a bookstore, you know something's wrong with your life.

I was snuggled into a puffy chair, focused on the book in my lap, Gretchen Rubin's *The Happiness Project*. It told the story of the author's yearlong journey to examine her life and make happiness-promoting changes recommended by scientists, philosophers, popular culture, and friends.

As I read the opening pages, I found myself nodding, relating to her ideas. She warned readers that her experience was unique, but I saw reflections of myself in her personality, her marriage style, and her interests. I read quickly and eagerly, thinking I could improve my life, too, and suddenly I was stirred by a long-forgotten feeling, hope.

When my husband and friend found me, I was a sniffling, emotional mess with tears soaking my cheeks. I was overwhelmed not only by a desire for change, but also the realization that I was ready to succeed. I pulled myself together and clutched the book possessively on my way to the checkout counter.

Over the next few weeks I savored the author's words, sometimes reading in bed or in a coffee shop, always with a pencil and paper nearby for notetaking. After I finished, I spent hours sitting at the desk in my study, designing my own happiness project. I considered what happiness meant to me and decided what behaviors to change or keep, how I would make that happen, and what attitudes I would cultivate. It looked like a lot to take on, but I had a plan. Getting more sleep, making time to relax with my husband, seeing my friends frequently—all these could be accomplished by better time management, right?

Not so fast. The moment I put my plan into action, I was immediately reminded that if it was all so easy, I'd have done it long ago. Sure, some changes were manageable, but I still only had twenty-four hours a day. If I wanted to expand time for my goals, I had to cut other priorities. How was I supposed to say no when everything was important?

Despite that struggle, life began to change—but not because I'd mastered time. I'll probably always wrestle with the clock. Instead things were looking up mainly because of two attitudes I embraced regardless of what was on my calendar: gratitude and presence.

Gratitude and I go way back. We're like old friends

who rarely see each other but always click when they do. Years ago, I'd started a gratitude journal, recording little joys like mint mochas and scented lotion as well as thankfulness for life-defining things like good health and loving relationships. At first I wrote often, then less so as time passed. I didn't give gratitude much thought until years later, when major surgery reminded me how much I needed it. There was nothing like being mostly helpless for months to remind me to appreciate the things I still could do.

The lessons of that time never left me, but, just like my attention to the journal, they faded into the background as life directed my attention elsewhere. It was time for another reminder.

I was running through my gym's parking lot during a rainstorm, preoccupied as usual. As I entered the gym, the desk clerk asked how I was.

"I'm soaked," I complained. "It's pouring out there!"

Instead of commiserating, he asked me an

unexpected question. "Do you like the rain?"

I was taken aback. Actually, I had always liked rain. I thought it was comforting, loved its sound, appreciated that it made everything so lushly green. Why was I complaining?

"Yeah, actually, I do," I said, feeling thankful he'd made me think about it. It was a simple moment, but it was an effective reminder that cultivating gratitude is like cultivating a friendship. The more effort I put into appreciating and acknowledging it, the more rewarded I feel.

To keep gratitude in my daily life, I started playing a game called "five things." I think of five things to be thankful for in the moment, with no generic answers allowed. Instead of "I'm grateful for my health," I'll say, "I'm grateful my leg feels well enough today to exercise." This game is particularly helpful when worry sidetracks me, such as when I'm driving home from my job, pointlessly dwelling on workday problems. To distract myself, I focus on five current things to be grateful for, for example, a project finished early, praise from my boss, a favorite song on the radio, a storybook-blue sky ideal for a late-afternoon walk, and the fact that my husband will be cooking his famously mouthwatering hamburgers that night.

Playing "five things," with its emphasis on what's right, right now, works well with its companion attitude—presence. It wasn't until I started making an effort to live in the moment that I realized how much time I'd spent fretting over past actions or worrying about future events. After struggling for years with anxiety, I was shocked to find that eliminating stress was often as simple as focusing on the present. You can't wander into traffic if you've stopped to smell the roses.

I discovered something delightful, too—like scissors cutting paper or rock crushing scissors, presence quashes worry. If I'm truly in the moment, I'm not worrying. I'm too busy taking action or having fun. If I start to worry, I can stop it by assigning a time to take the next step to solve the problem and then letting it go until it's time to act. If there's nothing I can do, I skip straight to letting it go. I've found it's not bad situations that sour my life, it's the related worrying that's most toxic.

I'm not saying I'm always happy. Interpreting my world through a prism of gratitude and presence takes practice, and sometimes I need reminders. Recently I was grumping around the house, knowing I should exercise but feeling uninspired. My right leg, which has periodically bothered me since my surgery, was aching.

"I need motivation help," I said to my husband, Frank, who had just gotten home from work. "Will you go on a walk with me?"

"I can't," he said. "My foot's hurting again, and I need to get off my feet."

I must have looked disappointed, because he glanced at me and said, "You look sad! You can't be sad! You're happy now, remember?"

I smiled at the fantasy that I could eliminate all unhappiness. Still, even as I complained that

I'd been putting off exercise for days, and you can't just do that—sure you can, the King of the Couch argued—my perspective was changing. Frank's comment reminded me that point of view is a decision I make. With that reminder, I knew I was going to walk. I'd appreciate the fresh air, the cold, clear sky, and my ability to take each step through the neighborhood. As I put on my walking shoes and my winter coat, I felt better already. Grateful. Happy.

~Alaina Smith

The Color of Happiness

*I would not waste my life in friction when it
could be turned into momentum.*
~Frances Willard

fter nine years of indecisiveness, I
finally decided to paint our home's
entryway and hallway. At least, "indecisiveness" was the explanation I gave.
But, looking around the other painted and decorated rooms of our home I finally realized there
were many other reasons it took me so long to
decide on a color for these supposedly welcoming
areas of our home.

Moving away from my hometown with my new husband, I had entered our home—a blank slate at the time as we were its first owners—feeling overwhelmed by the fact that I knew no one in this new town and had no idea how I would decorate the three bedrooms, two bathrooms, kitchen, breakfast nook, and living room. I so badly wanted our house to feel like a home, but at that time, it all felt so foreign—marriage, living on my own for the first time, a puppy. I was so terribly homesick, that for a little while, I was convinced that we would move back to my hometown and away from this overwhelming house.

Yet, over the next couple of years, our bedroom was painted, as was the bathroom (twice), the breakfast nook and kitchen (also twice), and ultimately our firstborn's room. Our son's room was beautiful, with a light green chair rail, light brown walls, jungle-themed bedding. His room was the most welcoming in the house. I always kept the entryway and hallway on my "to do" list, but our second baby (and beautiful room) and two jobs later, lack of time always seemed to be the excuse not to finish this project.

Over those years, my once close relationship with my parents cooled for a variety of reasons, their health began to decline, and their visits to my home became less frequent. The rejection stung, so to avoid feeling the pain of this loss, I busied myself with my children, housework, and other activities and put the entryway and hallway project on the back burner. It just seemed easier to do that than make a decision on paint — or to deal with my feelings.

After a couple of years, I realized I could no longer bury my feelings of rejection, hurt and loss, and sought the help of a counselor, who guided me through a process where I ultimately found happiness — and began to focus more inwardly on my own family, and less outwardly toward the family I once had.

And then one day, upon returning home from picking up my son from school, we walked into the house, and I realized how unwelcoming it looked to us—the white walls, the lack of pictures, and the lack of warm window coverings. It was as though—through the pain, rejection, depression and more—my feelings didn't allow me to take the final steps to making our house a home. It was as though I was waiting for my parents to tell me that they were planning to visit, and walk into that entryway again—which was the "perfect" excuse I was seeking to finally finish this project. But, my journey toward acceptance—accepting that my parents may never visit my home again, that I may never be fully accepted by them again, that my husband and children were the most important members of my family—finally revealed what I needed to do: paint away the past and look forward to a beautiful future with my family.

It seemed that my husband was just as excited about this final transition. He happily helped me paint over those white walls, removed the white blinds from the windows in preparation for warm colored curtains, and reveled in the transformation that our home underwent, with a simple coat of paint — "Harvest Brown." It was then that I realized that it didn't take me nine years to decide on a color — it took me nine years to finally look inside my home for happiness, and not outside of it.

~Heather McGowan

The Lucky One

*A daughter is the happy memories of the past,
the joyful moments of the present, and the
hope and promise of the future.*
~Author Unknown

ur daughter is a child of the Army. Her mother is an Army nurse; I am an Army lawyer—a "JAG" officer. Through three individual deployments to Afghanistan and Iraq I've learned that our greatest path to happiness is the unifying joy of our five-year-old, who over the course of many trials and separations continues to redeem us—she is what makes us lucky.

Emma was born in January 2006, during a

bitterly cold upstate New York winter, ten days before I deployed to Afghanistan. Five months later her mother was deployed there also. Emma landed, like so many other military children, with her grandparents, the youngest resident of the Bethany Village retirement community in Mechanicsburg, Pennsylvania, the ward of my eighty-six-year-old father and seventy-seven-year-old mother. She became one of the community's most popular residents, the instant delight of grandmothers and grandfathers alike, who are drawn to the youth and smiles of a five-month-old.

It is difficult to articulate the all-consuming guilt a parent feels when leaving an infant behind. It was particularly hard on her mother. Of course we chose this life, despite its inconveniences and separations, out of a genuine belief that military service was something that mattered—to be part of the large moral reserve where values like sacrifice, honor, selflessness, and integrity still matter. Our fidelity to those values would be dearly tested. If you have ever left a baby behind for a combat zone… well, it just isn't easy.

I returned from Bagram and Kandahar eight months later to reclaim a child I hardly knew, and was arguably unqualified to care for without some sort of adult supervision. It was Emma, me, and two Wheaten Terriers, 370 miles from the nearest family member. I will forever be grateful for the support from my boss's wife who graciously checked in, providing advice such as not to feed hot dogs to an eight-month-old, and otherwise made sure I didn't do anything shockingly stupid.

And yet, despite the endless days, the bottles and diapers, the lost weekends and sleepless nights, missed meetings and a worn-out BlackBerry, I ended each long day feeling as though something meaningful had happened between Emma and me. We survived, we thrived, and we would wake up the next morning to do it all over again. In truth, I felt almost indescribably lucky for the time alone with her.

So each night from those days forward, while we awaited her mother's return from Afghanistan the following year, I would look down in utter amazement at this gorgeous daughter of mine and quietly ask her, "Why am I lucky?" And then I would softly answer, "Because I have you." I had Emma. Mom was a world away. The family was a day's drive away. In the cold and snowy Watertown winter of 2006-2007 it was just the two of us and the dogs. Looking back it was one of the most indelibly memorable periods of my life.

Over time, as Emma learned to talk, she gradually picked up the refrain. I still remember the exact moment, lying in bed after *Click Clack Moo* and *If You Give a Mouse a Cookie*, that she rolled over and said, "Dad, you're lucky because you have me." Indeed I was.

It has been, and I am ever prayerful that it will always be, one of the heartfelt narratives of our relationship: the simple but sublime acknowledgement that I am fortunate because of the blessing of my daughter in my life and her awareness of how I feel about us; what we had, and what we shall always have.

I am lucky because throughout the preschool age of princesses she always allowed me to be her prince; she would dress up in a rotating collection of about a dozen dresses, glass slippers and all, and we would dance through the house as she sang theme songs from *Beauty and the Beast* and *Cinderella* with joyous abandon.

I am lucky because Emma inspires and fortifies me to be more than I am: a window on a world I never fully imagined before she came into my life. In the early days when it was just the two of us, and ever since, I wake up early as much for her as for myself. Fatherhood brought a new imperative to support and provide and make something of this life so she can be proud. She is the high school coach we all ran an extra mile for because the victories were for him as much as us—a coach in size 3 slippers and a Hello Kitty nightgown with a laugh that melts whatever egocentricities remain in her father.

I am lucky because she unifies us as a family. Emma is the connective tissue that brings purpose to the sometimes tumultuous rhythm of our lives. She reinforces the relationship that brought her into the world, sustains it with meaning, and focuses it on the future.

On about her fourth birthday the old refrain added a new line. "Why am I lucky?" I would ask. "Because you have me," she quietly responded. Then to my surprise came the question, "Dad, why am I lucky?"

"I don't know sugar bear, why?"

"Because I have you, Dad. Because I have all of you."

But the lucky one... the really, truly, lucky recipient of the magic that is our father/daughter love affair, is me. She is the lantern that guides my feet along the path of happiness. One day she will find that prince and hopefully know the utter joy of little fingers wrapped tightly around her own hand.

And the magic will continue through her. Lucky until the end.

~*Colonel George R. Smawley*

The Happy Book

*Every day may not be good, but there's
something good in every day.*
~Author Unknown

I've spent a lot of my life unhappy. Looking
back there were times that it was okay to feel
that way, for example when my parents got
divorced, when I was mugged at gunpoint
during a vacation, when two friends died in a car
accident when I was in high school, and when I
was brutally assaulted in my early twenties.

But there were the other times, too. In middle
school I didn't think that I was as smart as everyone
else; I didn't have cool enough clothes; my mother
dropped me off at school in a beat-up car. Junior

high was the same. I wasn't as tall and thin as all the other girls; my baby teeth hadn't fallen out yet; and where were my boobs? Fast forward to high school. Still the boys had eyes for others; still everyone was smarter; still everyone dressed better. Yes, my boobs had finally arrived, but somehow that paled in comparison to everything else. In my first job out of college I wasn't making as much money as my friends; my apartment wasn't as nice; when I looked around there was always something to feel miserable about.

I come from a long line of people who have suffered from diagnosable depression. When I was single, I assumed that was just who I was—it was the genes I had been dealt.

When I was twenty-four I met my husband. We got married three years later, and three years after that I had my first child.

Once we had kids, my excuse of "it's-in-the-genes" didn't work so well for me anymore because that meant my kids were going to be depressed. And although I realize that that still might be the case, I began looking at my unhappiness in a new way.

It was something I had to work on myself.

Over the years many things have helped me fight depression: healthy eating, exercise, fresh air, friends, volunteering, church, therapy and medicine. It all helps.

But I have a little secret, too.

It's an exercise that I do every night before bed. By the side of my bed I have a small datebook. It covers January to December, but it's small—every day only has enough space to write one line.

Every night I ask myself this question: "What made me the happiest today?"

Because I don't have space to write very much it seems easy, and it only takes me a few seconds. But in those seconds I replay my day and decide on its happiest moment. Some days I come up with answers I expect, and other days I find myself surprised.

Some days it's: "my husband came home early," "reading before bed with the kids," "laughing with a friend on the phone," "getting a parking space when I was late… right in front!"

And some days aren't as easy and it's: "finally getting to get into bed," "being able to stay calm during a fight with my daughter," "not having to cook dinner—again."

But the spin on my life has changed. I actively seek the positive. Every day.

And sometimes, if I have a sour day, I look back through the book, read, and remember those happy moments in the past.

In fact, I wish I had started my happy book back in middle school. Entries might have been: "I don't need braces like everyone else," "I caught Charlie S. looking at me today," and "I didn't trip when I went up on stage to receive my Most Improved Player award."

~*Jennifer Quasha*

Asperger's and Friendship

A friend is someone who understands your
past, believes in your future, and accepts
you just the way you are.
~Author Unknown

As far back as I can remember I was the odd one out at school and for me it meant a lack of friends. However, those who were willing to be my friends tried to help me, and I had a core group of friends who stuck with me through the storms of elementary, junior high and high school.

When I was diagnosed with Asperger's syndrome

in the ninth grade, I was told that I would have to go to a special school for autistic kids. My resource teacher at that time said it would be a bad idea, and then he asked me if it was okay for him to talk to my class about my diagnosis. For those who do not know what Asperger's syndrome is, it is a high functioning form of autism characterized by a special interest, sensory integration dysfunction, lack of social skills, communications, and executive function.

I thought we were giving them more ammunition with which to tease me. Well, I was mistaken. Instead, they rallied around me, teaching me what was socially acceptable and how to study better.

I wound up being on the Academic Decathlon team for three years; in my senior year I was team captain. I helped lead the team to Most Improved and received the Most Inspirational Participant award. But I will never forget the high point of senior year—I was asked to be a starting player at the senior alum game; when I went on court my peers started to stamp their feet and call out my name. The game was slowed down, and I was passed the ball. When I missed the first shot, my peers stamped harder and called my name louder. I landed the second shot and scored two points. I will never forget the cheering of my peers. I was voted MVP even though I had scored only two points.

When I moved on to college I found another group of friends at the University of La Verne and these friends have been with me now for five years. I will never forget their kindness. As an Aspie, I don't deal well with surprises; I need to rehearse possible scenarios. But on my twenty-second birthday my university friends decorated the door and hallway of my dorm. I was overcome by the surprise, but surprisingly, I didn't have a meltdown from the surprise! They surprised me again on my twenty-fourth birthday.

But the real moment I found happiness, and really understood what was meant by happiness and friendship, was yesterday — April 9, 2011. It was a joint birthday party for me, my cousin who I call my big sister, and her sister's boyfriend. I had invited thirteen people and only five showed up, but the five that came included an old friend from elementary school, a friend and mentor from high school, and two friends from the university. I was nervous and scared because I had no idea what to expect, but when the party was over I had received a true gift. I realized what makes me happy and stronger is having a large group of friends. Just having a friend is highly unusual for someone with Asperger's, but I have a large support group: a core of five friends that have stayed in contact since elementary school; a group from secondary school, and now friends from the university.

I have two other friends with the same diagnosis and they don't have friends like I do — friends who support me, who guide me, and who are not afraid to tell me when I have done something incorrectly.

My friends make me happy, and they make my life worth living—because I am rich in friends.

~Richard Nakai

Happiness Is
Being a Parent

*Happiness often sneaks in through a
door you didn't know you left open.*
~John Barrymore

The thing that stood out about my family was the fighting. My mother was a fierce, volatile, and determined woman who insisted on being right. When I was five, she left my father in Hong Kong and brought me to the U.S. to start a new life. My stepfather was so emotionally wounded as a child that he lied about his age to join the Navy in order to escape his family. He dealt with his pain by plunging himself into a sea of alcohol. While growing up, I witnessed these two in knockdown, drag-outs that made the Ali/Frazier bouts seem like polite tea parties.

I learned from my family that I shouldn't have kids; I didn't have a clue how to be a parent. My mother and stepfather showed me the devastation two people could inflict on each other, and the thought of doing that to my children scared the hell out of me. Besides, who needed that kind of responsibility? So I bailed on the whole concept of being a parent. Deep down, I was afraid I'd be a miserable failure in the most important role anyone could undertake—raising a child.

My wife, Quyen, and I dated two years before getting married. Throughout the course of our relationship, I told her I didn't want to be a father, and she never tried to change my mind. Still, I understood her desire to be a mother. She came from Vietnam and lived through the horror of the Vietnam War. In the aftermath, her family lost their home, the restaurant business that supported them, and all their possessions to the Communist government. All they had left was each other.

Quyen grew up in a family of eight children and helped take care of her siblings. She cherished the role. Her dream in coming to America was to start a family so she could raise her own kids, yet she still married me knowing my stand on being a parent. This thought always leaves me humbled beyond words.

I remember the day my life changed. Quyen and I attended a friend's party. Among the guests happened to be a couple with a baby boy. When my wife caught sight of him, she lit up like the angel atop a Christmas tree. She asked to hold the infant and gently cradled him, her expression of unadulterated joy readily apparent at the bundle of life gurgling in her arms.

Quyen stayed with the baby as his parents mingled, and I marveled at how he gazed into her eyes while she sang lullabies. She dabbed dribble from his mouth with a Kleenex. When he cried, she retrieved a bottle from his mom, fed him, and patted his back until he burped. My wife was utterly enraptured. I watched her slowly rock the baby to sleep, his head nestled upon her shoulder like a kitten on its mother's belly.

I made a decision that night; I would be a father. I still didn't trust myself to do it right, but I knew Quyen would more than make up for my shortcomings. When we arrived home after the party, I conveyed this to Quyen, and let's just say a child's first glimpse of Disneyland wouldn't have held a candle to the radiance bursting forth from my wife. She pulled me to her and cried the kind of deep, sobbing tears that well up from the core of your being when you experience something that truly matters.

After a time, Quyen clasped my hands as if to impart meaning through her touch. Then she looked at me with an unwavering smile. The sureness in her eyes communicated to me before she spoke.

"You're going to be a great father," she said.

Today, we are blessed to have ten-year-old Kevin and seven-year-old Kristie in our lives. We named our son after Kevin Costner because Quyen and I loved *Dances with Wolves*. Kristi Yamaguchi's grace and artistry on the ice gave us the inspiration for our daughter's name.

Kevin can spend hours on his Nintendo DS Lite, Wii, or anything video game related. Quyen and I have to set strict guidelines or he'd be playing 24/7. He's a chatterbox who can't get enough company. His favorite food is Kirkland macaroni and cheese. He is so sensitive that his eyes tear up when his cousin from Hawaii departs after staying with us for a week.

Once, Quyen and I were discussing our ideal careers at the dinner table and I asked Kevin what he wanted to be when he grows up. My son thought for a moment before proclaiming in complete earnestness, "I want to be a free man. That way I can stay home and play games with my kids all the time."

Kristie snuggles next to me as I read her children's books. She unleashes a lilting medley of exasperation if I don't tell her a bedtime story every night. She teases me by pretending to fall asleep in the car whenever we are driving home from Costco. Her favorite food is microwaved chicken nuggets. When I'm feeling down, she somehow senses it and spends time with me. My funk immediately disappears.

Kristie asked me a question last week. "Daddy, there's a Father's Day and a Mother's Day. How come we don't have a Kid's Day?"

To say my children mean the universe to me is an understatement. Put simply, they give my life a purpose and I thank the heavens each and every day for the two most precious gifts a father could ever receive.

~Ray M. Wong

Happy New Year

*Patience is the ability to count
down before you blast off.*
~Author Unknown

There they were. Two pink lines… on my home pregnancy test. It was confirmed: I was pregnant. This wasn't exactly news I could sit on, despite the fact that it was a quarter past six in the morning. I had initially ventured into the bathroom to take a closer look at our humidifier, which appeared to be on the blink.

I padded back to bed with bare feet, crawled across the bed, and nudged my husband, Scott, who was snoring and motionless under more than his fair share of the comforter.

"Babe," I began, prodding him relentlessly, "two things: the humidifier is indeed broken…"

Not surprisingly, this declaration didn't elicit a response.

"…and we're pregnant," I finished.

That one, however, did the trick.

Scott awoke with a start and switched on the lamp, his eyes wide and inquisitive. "Really?" And then his mouth formed into a large smile.

I proudly scurried back to the bathroom to produce the evidence, brought it to the bedroom, and showed Scott.

His smile cooled. "The line is… really light," he said with a hint of disbelief.

"Light still means pregnant," I replied in my best I-am-too-pregnant tone.

"Hmmm, I don't know," he said, planting a hint of doubt inside my own head.

Cut to the office of our family doctor two hours later. Scott had an appointment for a routine check-up, and he had goaded me into coming along so that the nurse, Sherry, could give me a blood test.

"Exciting!" Sherry exclaimed as she withdrew the needle from my arm. "I'm off tomorrow, so the next time I talk to you, maybe…" her voice trailed off into a roller coaster of anticipatory squeals. "This is going to the lab today. Call back tomorrow morning. The results will definitely be in by 10 a.m."

But they weren't. I checked. Twice. Then I spent an inordinate amount of time pondering what could have possibly come between my test results and their timely — promised! — delivery to my doctor's office. Not knowing was doing a number on my already shaky conviction.

Maybe I wasn't pregnant.

That day, my yoga practice saved me from was-I-or-wasn't-I limbo. I deliberately lost myself in an invigorating self-practice at home, and then I drove to a friend's home to teach her privately. This brought me back down to earth, and the benefits were twofold: It was preparation for the upcoming final exam in my yoga instructor training program, and it served to calm my nerves by reminding me to live in the moment. This moment.

The next day, New Year's Eve to be exact, I tried the doctor's office again. I was equipped with a level head, but my breath caught in my throat when an unfamiliar, albeit chipper, female voice filtered through the line. "Good morning, how may I help you?"

"Yes, my name is Courtney Conover, and I'm calling to obtain the results of my pregnancy test," I said, the rising intonation of my voice surely disclosing my hopefulness.

"Please hold."

It had been a full forty-eight hours. The results had to be there. As I held the phone, a parade of never-before-experienced milestones ran through my head: What I would look like with a swollen belly; Scott and I bringing our baby home from the hospital; our child opening presents on Christmas morning.

And then the proverbial needle scratched the record.

"Hi, Courtney? Um, yeah, well, the results are here… but we can't give them to you. You see, the doctor must be in to verify them, and he won't be back until Monday. Sorry."

I had hit the nadir. My stomach gave a lurch and then immediately began turning about as if on spin cycle. This couldn't be. Wasn't it inhumane to expect a possibly pregnant woman to remain in left field about her status? On New Year's Eve of all days? I wanted to proclaim this—no, shout it—but an imperfect combination of shock and outrage choked back my words. I hung up.

Frustrated and nearly incoherent, I then dialed Scott at work. Scott, bless his heart, calmed me down and said that he'd call the doctor's office to see what on earth could be done.

In the meantime, I had to get my act together so that I could go to work myself: I was bringing my mother along to a burning bowl ceremony I was covering for my weekly column, and it was set to start in thirty minutes.

Consider the irony: I fancied myself a positive thinker; I was this close to becoming a yoga teacher so that I could help others live healthier, more peaceful lives; and I was en route to a burning bowl ceremony, a ritual that encouraged people to let go of old, unproductive thought patterns in order to make room for useful, promising ones. Yet here I was, fit to be tied over something beyond my control—despite having so many blessings in my life.

And the cherry on top?

There was still a chance that I could have been pregnant.

I spent the next three hours among a wonderful group of men and women who wanted nothing more than to make 2011 bigger, better—happier—than the year that preceded it. The moderator gave us two sheets of paper, one for writing down things we wanted to release and another for writing down what we wanted to attract into our lives. It was a powerful exercise, one that shed enormous light on all that I already had to be thankful for: my health; a loving husband; a supportive mother; the ability to pursue my passion as a writer. My list, admittedly, was rather long. If that wasn't reason enough to be happy in the new year, I didn't know what was.

Still, I could think of something I needed to let go: My fervent desire for things to always go the way I wanted.

I consider it more than coincidence that my day started looking up after the ceremony. As soon as my mother and I entered my car, my cell phone's voicemail alert chimed; it was Scott. I felt a frisson of excitement as I called him back. Maybe—just maybe—he had some news.

He did: I was pregnant.

Scott had somehow contacted Sherry, who had somehow reached the doctor so that he could give the aforementioned clearance.

So, there, on a rainy New Year's Eve, in the

parking lot of the burning bowl ceremony, with my mother by my side and my husband on the phone, I learned that I was expecting my first child.

At that moment, absolutely nothing else mattered. Talk about putting the happy in Happy New Year.

~Courtney Conover

Meet Our Contributors

Courtney Conover is a writer and yogini who resides in Michigan with her husband, Scott. And this fall, baby makes three: Their first child, Scotty Jr., is due in September. This is Courtney's fifth contribution to the *Chicken Soup for the Soul* series. Visit her online at www.courtneyconover.com.

Ruth Jones lives in Cookeville, TN, with her husband Terry and a very fat cat named Annabel.

Debra Mayhew is a pastor's wife and home-schooling mom to six children. After faith and family, her greatest passion is writing for children. Debra loves good books, long walks, and an empty laundry basket. E-mail her at debra@debramayhew.com or visit www.debramayhew.com to learn more.

Heather McGowan is a wife, mother of two young children, and owner of Sounding Board Marketing & Communications in Folsom, CA. Read Heather's blogs about her experiences as a working mother on hvmcgowanmakingendsmeet.blogspot.com.

Richard Nakai is a graduate of the University of La Verne. His interests include Japanese history and European medieval history. He has two cats named Shadow and Tama. Richard is an Aspie. E-mail him at rulerofworld14@hotmail.com.

Jennifer Quasha has been a freelance writer and editor since 1998, and she loves to write for the *Chicken Soup for the Soul* series. When she's not writing, editing, or reading, you'll find her chasing after her human and canine family members, or asleep. Learn more at www.jenniferquasha.com and www. smallpawsbarefeet.com.

Angela Sayers was a twenty-year-old cancer patient who sought to raise awareness for pediatric cancers, especially osteosarcoma. She loved books, writing, playing online *Scrabble*, and her cat, Charles Fitzpatrick The Third.

Colonel George Smawley is an officer in the U.S. Army Judge Advocate General's Corps. He wrote "The Lucky One" while serving in Iraq with the 25th Infantry Division. He received his B.A. in English from Dickinson College, and his J.D. from the Temple University School of Law.

Alaina Smith loves a good story. Her true tales appear in multiple anthologies including two other *Chicken Soup for the Soul* books, six *Chocolate for Women* books, five *A Cup of Comfort* books, and more.

She enjoys writing, working for a musical theater company, and moviegoing with her husband, Frank.

Ray M. Wong is devoted to his wife, Quyen. He cherishes his children, Kevin and Kristie. Ray is studying creative non-fiction in the MFA program at Antioch University Los Angeles. He is working on a memoir about a journey to Hong Kong that changed his life. Visit him at www.raywong.info or e-mail ray@raywong.info.

Meet Amy Newmark

Amy Newmark is the bestselling author, editor-in-chief, and publisher of the *Chicken Soup for the Soul* book series. Since 2008, she has published 140 new books, most of them national bestsellers in the U.S. and Canada, more than doubling the number of Chicken Soup for the Soul titles in print today. She is also the author of *Simply Happy*, a crash course in Chicken Soup for the Soul advice and wisdom that is filled with easy-to-implement, practical tips for having a better life.

Amy is credited with revitalizing the Chicken

Soup for the Soul brand, which has been a publishing industry phenomenon since the first book came out in 1993. By compiling inspirational and aspirational true stories curated from ordinary people who have had extraordinary experiences, Amy has kept the twenty-four-year-old Chicken Soup for the Soul brand fresh and relevant.

Amy graduated *magna cum laude* from Harvard University where she majored in Portuguese and minored in French. She then embarked on a three-decade career as a Wall Street analyst, a hedge fund manager, and a corporate executive in the technology field. She is a Chartered Financial Analyst.

Her return to literary pursuits was inevitable, as her honors thesis in college involved traveling throughout Brazil's impoverished northeast region, collecting stories from regular people. She is delighted to have come full circle in her writing career — from collecting stories "from the people" in Brazil as a twenty-year-old to, three decades later, collecting stories "from the people" for Chicken Soup for the Soul.

When Amy and her husband Bill, the CEO of Chicken Soup for the Soul, are not working, they are visiting their four grown children.

Follow Amy on Twitter @amynewmark. Listen to her free daily podcast, The Chicken Soup for the Soul Podcast, at www.chickensoup.podbean.com, or find it on iTunes, the Podcasts app on iPhone, or on your favorite podcast app on other devices.

Changing lives one story at a time®
www.chickensoup.com